**DO NOT REMOVE
CARDS FROM POCKET**

2/97

**ALLEN COUNTY PUBLIC LIBRARY
FORT WAYNE, INDIANA 46802**

You may return this book to any agency, branch,

or bookmobile of the Allen County Public Library.

DEMCO

IMAGES

Texture

Karen Bryant-Mole

Silver Press
Parsippany, New Jersey

First published in Great Britain by Heinemann Library, an imprint of
Heinemann Publishers (Oxford) Ltd., Halley Court, Jordan Hill, Oxford OX2 8EJ, U.K.

© BryantMole Books 1996

Designed by Jean Wheeler
Commissioned photography by Zul Mukhida
Printed in Hong Kong

00 99 98 97 96
10 9 8 7 6 5 4 3 2 1

Published in the United States in 1997 by Silver Press
A Division of Simon & Schuster
299 Jefferson Road
Parsippany, NJ 07054

Library of Congress Cataloging-in-Publication Data

Bryant-Mole, Karen.
  Texture/by Karen Bryant-Mole.
    p.   cm. — (Images)
  Includes index.
    Summary: Photographs as well as simple text introduce a variety of textures such as wet
(a glass of orange juice), ridged (corduroy), and scaly (reptile skin).
  ISBN 0-382-39585-9 (LSB)—ISBN 0-382-39621-9 (PBK)
    1. Materials—Texture—Juvenile literature. [1. Touch. 2. Senses and sensations.] I. Title.
II. Series: Bryant-Mole, Karen.
  TA403.2.B79   1996   95-48063
  602.1'1292—dc20   CIP
                                                                              AC

Allen County Public Library
900 Webster Street
PO Box 2270
Fort Wayne, IN 46801-2270

Some of the more difficult words in this book are explained in the glossary.

Acknowledgments
The Publishers would like to thank the following for permission to reproduce photographs. Oxford Scientific Films,
16 (right); Gordon A Maclean, 17 (right); Kathie Atkinson, 23 (top); Max Gibbs, Tony Stone Images, 16 (left); Marc
Chamberlain, 22 (left), 23 (bottom); Art Wolfe, 22 (right); Rod Planck, Zefa, 17 (left).

Every effort had been made to contact copyright holders of any material reproduced in this book. Any omissions will be
rectified in subsequent printings if notice is given to the Publisher.

Contents

Smooth objects feel flat.

Can you find
some more
smooth objects?

5

Rough

These things feel rough.

a shell

some bark

a cheese
grater

a broken brick

Soft

Soft toys feel nice
to cuddle.

Soft clothes feel comfortable
to wear.

Hard

Most hard objects do not bend.

Would these
things feel
nice to cuddle?

11

Wet

All these things feel wet.

bubble mixture

orange juice

paints

tomato
ketchup

13

Dry

None of these things feel wet.

They all feel dry.

Spiky

Spiky things often
have prickles.

Many plants and animals use spikes
to protect themselves.

Knobbly

Knobbly
objects are
covered in lumps
and bumps.

18

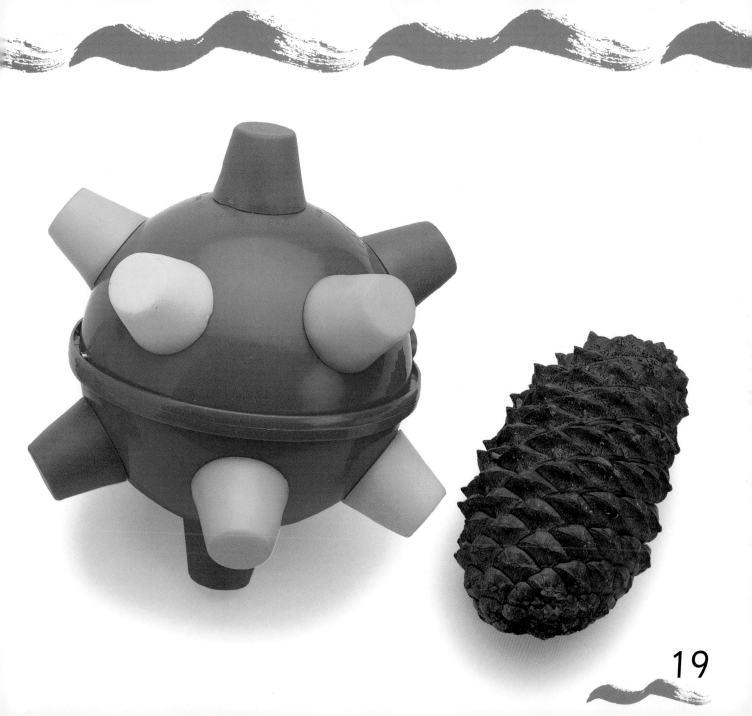

19

Ridged

Objects with raised lines feel ridged.

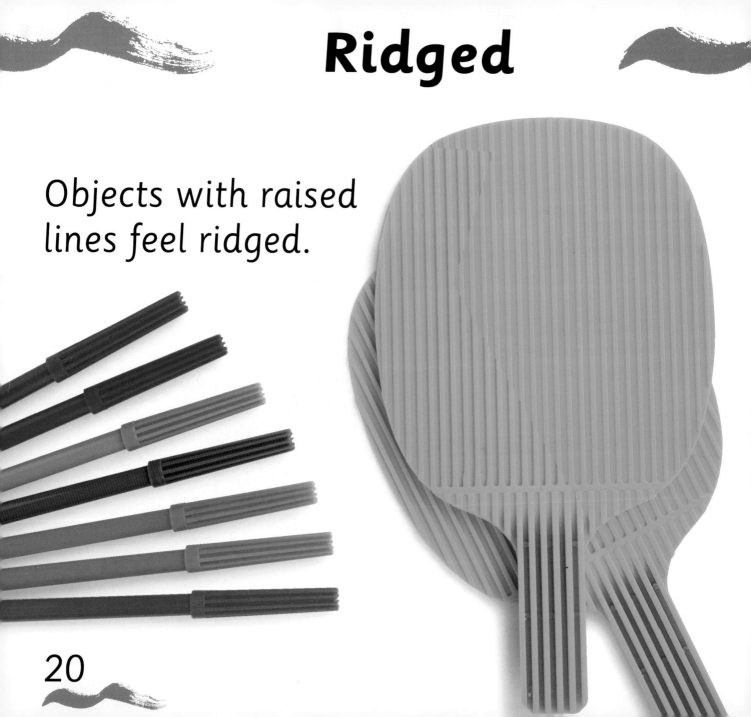

Fabric can feel
ridged, too!

21

Scaly

Many fish and reptiles are scaly.

The thin,
overlapping
scales protect
their skins.

Glossary

bark the outside layer of a tree's trunk
overlapping to rest on top of something and
  partly cover it up
protect keep safe
raised sticking up

Index